7.98

D1199090

A BOOK OF VERSE

A BOOK OF VERSE

A facsimile of the manuscript
written in 1870 by

WILLIAM MORRIS

Clarkson N. Potter, Inc./Publishers

DISTRIBUTED BY CROWN PUBLISHERS, INC.

NEW YORK

Copyright © 1980 by Scolar Press
All rights reserved. No part of this book may be reproduced or transmitted in any form or by any means, electronic or mechanical, including photocopying, recording, or by any information storage and retrieval system, without permission in writing from the publisher.

Published in the United States by Clarkson N. Potter, Inc., One Park Avenue, New York, New York 10016 and simultaneously in Canada by General Publishing Company Limited

Published in Great Britain in 1981 by Scolar Press
Manufactured in Great Britain

Library of Congress Cataloging in Publication Data
Morris, William, 1834–1896.
A book of verse.
Reprint. Originally published: London: Scolar Press, 1981.
Bibliography: p.
1. Morris, William, 1834–1896—Manuscripts—Facsimiles.
I. Title.
PR5078.B6 1982 821'.8 82-13152
ISBN 0-517-549026

10 9 8 7 6 5 4 3 2 1
First American Edition

Contents

The Morris and Burne-Jones families;
a photograph taken by William Hollyer between 1875 and 1880.
From left to right,
front: Georgiana Burne-Jones, Jenny Morris, Margaret Burne-Jones, Janey Morris, May Morris;
back: Philip Burne-Jones, Edward Burne-Jones's father, Edward Burne-Jones, William Morris.

William Morris 1834-1896

by Dr Roy Strong, Director, Victoria and Albert Museum

The life of William Morris spanned almost the whole of the Victorian period, but he himself was anything but a Victorian; indeed many would consider that his influence was greatest in the twentieth century. His active enquiring mind led him to take an interest in a variety of arts and crafts, some long neglected, as well as in the social and economic conditions of the day. Morris's interests never remained passive – he had always to find out for himself, to try his own hand, to participate and to share. This book is symptomatic of his attitude in many ways, especially in its shared responsibility and active participation. But it also meant something very special for Morris's personal life.

William Morris and Edward Burne-Jones had been close friends since they had met as undergraduates at Oxford. When they married, their families continued the same intimate companionship for some years. But by the late 1860s both marriages were in disarray. Janey Morris was becoming more and more involved with Dante Gabriel Rossetti; and Burne-Jones had become infatuated with Marie Zambaco. Morris, suffering emotionally himself, could feel for the similar sufferings endured by Georgiana Burne-Jones ('Georgy') and *A Book of Verse* reveals much of his innermost feelings at this period. The poems include some that appear to refer directly to his relationship with Georgy at a time when they were so closely drawn together; there is an underlying sadness for what is past, and for an unfulfilled love. There is no doubt that Morris derived great satisfaction in writing out his own poems for Georgy and putting all his art into fashioning a beautiful object to contain the expression of his emotions, which were usually so carefully concealed from prying eyes. The result of this complete involvement of Morris's personal life and his art was the production of a unique manuscript made for the pleasure of the woman with whom he shared much sorrow and love.

William Morris in 1874, a photograph by William Hollyer.

Georgiana Burne-Jones, by Edward Poynter RA. Private collection.

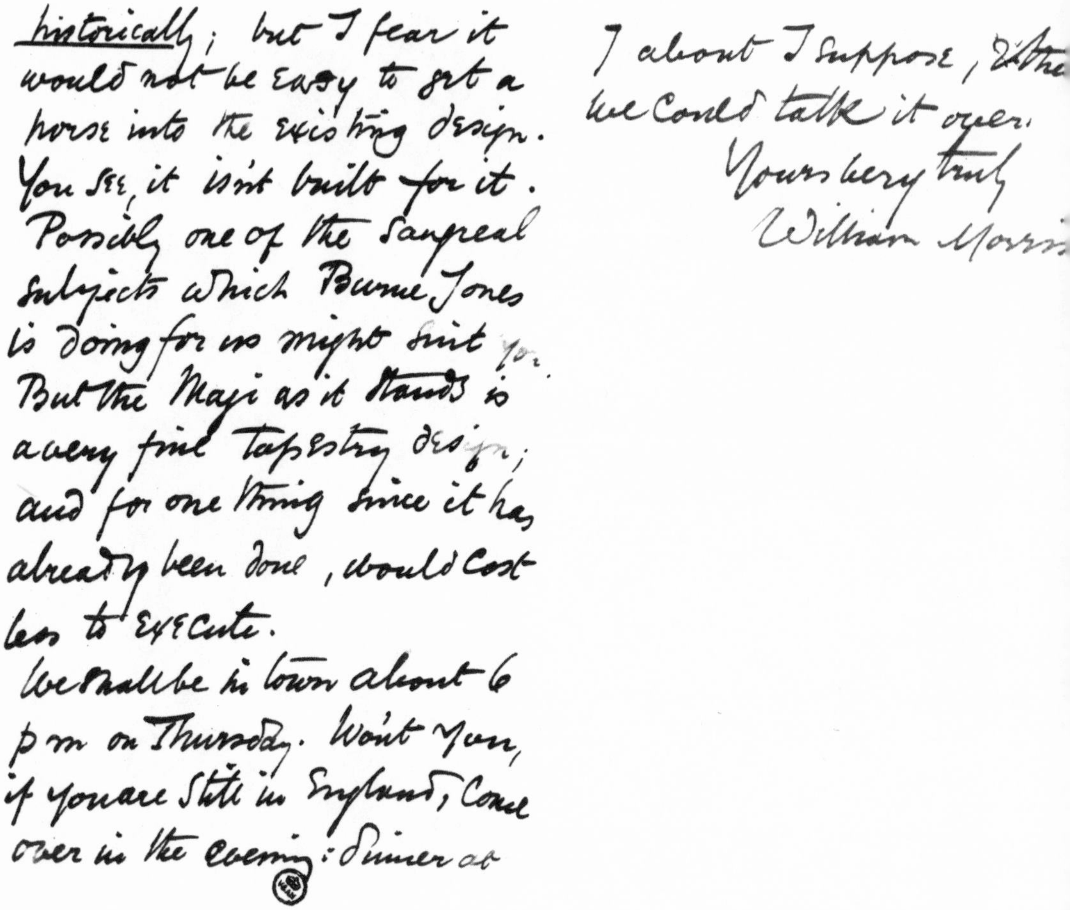

historically; but I fear it would not be easy to get a horse into the existing design. You see, it isn't built for it. Possibly one of the Sangreal subjects which Burne Jones is doing for us might suit you. But the Magi as it stands is a very fine tapestry design; and for one thing since it has already been done, would cost less to execute.

We shall be in town about 6 p m on Thursday. Won't you, if you are still in England, come over in the evening: dinner at

7 about I suppose, & the[n] we could talk it over.

Yours very truly
William Morri[s]

A specimen of William Morris's usual handwriting, taken from one of the letters to Wilfred Scawen Blunt, written after 1885. (Reduced)

William Morris: A Book of Verse 1870

by Joyce Irene Whalley, Assistant Keeper of the Library, Victoria and Albert Museum

A Book of Verse by William Morris appeared in a sale at Sotheby's, London, on 22 December 1952, as Lot 99. The description of this sale stated that it contained 'valuable printed books, autograph letters and historical documents etc.', and that the contents were partly selected from the library of Mrs J. W. Mackail, including 'material inherited from her parents, the late Sir Edward Burne-Jones, Bart., and Lady Burne-Jones'. The manuscript had thus remained in the family until it was purchased at the sale by the Victoria and Albert Museum, with the help of the Friends of the National Libraries. Mrs Mackail was Margaret Burne-Jones before her marriage, and her husband was the biographer of William Morris; his work is still the standard account of that remarkable man, his activities and his circle. The manuscript thus acquired by the Library of the Victoria and Albert Museum was produced by William Morris for the birthday of Lady Burne-Jones (then Mrs Burne-Jones) in August 1870. It was written on paper, ornamented with painted designs, and bound in vellum by Rivière with a design of gold fleurons on both covers.

It was not surprising that among his many other interests William Morris should have found time to produce so demanding a work as this manuscript book. Since his youth he had been fascinated by medieval illuminated manuscripts, and during his undergraduate days he had studied the manuscripts in the Bodleian Library, Oxford. He was very conscious of the many skills which had gone to the making of the finished manuscript – or indeed of any early book – and in time he tried his hand at all of them. It was undoubtedly this study of early manuscripts which subsequently influenced his printed books. But it was not easy for anyone, however enthusiastic, to recreate the art of the medieval scribe and illuminator in the second half of the nineteenth century, since the basic skills had been largely forgotten. Moreover, there had been considerable changes in writing equipment which made it almost impossible, at the time when Morris made his first attempts, to reproduce the exact effects of the medieval scribe. The paper (where this was used in preference to vellum) had a different texture, the composition of the inks had changed, and, above all, by the 1860s the steel pen had largely replaced the traditional quill. But there did exist a very real interest in the production of 'medieval' illuminated books, and in this

Morris was typical of his generation. With the advent of a commercially viable method of colour printing, there issued during the 1860s and 1870s a stream of manuals on the art of illuminating, mainly aimed at the amateur.

Morris, however, was not one of the amateur band, in this or in any other of his projects. He did his best to imitate exactly the workings of the medieval artists and craftsmen whom he so greatly admired. According to his daughter, May Morris, he made detailed studies of manuscripts in the British Museum, making voluminous notes and sketches in his pocket books. Morris's usual handwriting was bold and sprawling and he needed to evolve a completely different script for his manuscript work. Inevitably he was most influenced in the first instance by gothic letters, but by about 1870 (the date of *A Book of Verse*), he had formulated a very characteristic hand which owed something to the copy books of sixteenth-century Italy, and this script he used henceforward in all his manuscript works.

When it came to illuminating and decorating a book, Morris was on much surer ground. Not only could he use his own eyes to study medieval manuscripts, but there also survived medieval texts on illuminating which he could read and implement. May Morris recalls his work table: 'there was precious ultramarine in a slim cake, there was pale gold in shells, and gold leaf in books .... We were shown how the gold was laid .... Then there was the beautifully white vellum .... and quill pens ....' It was about 1870 when Morris took up illuminating seriously, and the birthday gift of *A Book of Verse* for Georgiana Burne-Jones was his first important venture. This manuscript, although deriving its inspiration from medieval sources, was not so much an illuminated work as a painted one, although titles and headings were in gold. The book is a decorated book – decorated with leaves and flowers that twine up the margins and interlace themselves into the text of the poems: 'a tangle of swift delicate pen-work in brown with leafage and flowers lightly painted in thin colour' is how May Morris describes this work, so redolent of early summer. Indeed the extreme delicacy of the paint-and-pen-work in this manuscript can never have been more fully appreciated than when the production of the facsimile was under consideration. As the twentieth-century craftsmen peered at the work under a magnifying glass, they despaired of ever matching up to the fine quality and detail of the original. The beauty of the colouring, with all its subtlety, and the intricacies of hairlines and dots which decorate the foliage, have proved as much a test of book making as anything Morris could have experienced in his own printing experiments.

Morris had not intended to do all the book work himself, allocating various parts of it to his friends and fellow-workers, as had been done among medieval craftsmen. The manuscript contains a portrait of Morris himself on the title-page, painted by Charles Fairfax Murray from the photograph profile of 1870, and it was Fairfax Murray who did all the rest of the pictures, with the exception of the one on page 1, which was by Burne-Jones. As for the pattern work, George Wardle drew all the ornament on the first ten pages, and Morris coloured it; Wardle also did all the coloured letters, but Morris himself executed the rest of the ornament 'together with all the writing'. It is perhaps fortunate for us that Morris added all this information in the colophon to the manuscript, since stylistically all the artists were very much akin, though a detailed study of the various parts can reveal the individual hands.

Of the texts of the manuscript, Morris wrote 'Also I made all the verses', but, he adds hastily, 'two poems . . . . I translated out of Icelandic' – as if he felt that he should disclaim the originality of these verses which in fact he has made very much his own. A number of poems in *A Book of Verse* were subsequently published in *Poems by the Way*. This work was first issued by the Kelmscott Press in 1891, but some of the poems had already appeared in various journals. However, the versions which Morris chose to write out for Georgiana Burne-Jones were not always those which appeared in print, and it can be an interesting exercise for the reader to discover the variations in the manuscript and printed texts, and to analyse the reasons for the changes. Titles too could vary. The poem called 'Missing' in the manuscript had been 'The Dark Wood' on its first appearance in *The Fortnightly* for February 1871, but was re-titled 'Error and Loss' in *Poems by the Way*.

A Book of Verse by William Morris therefore displays all the varied abilities of this versatile artist-craftsman – as he would have wished to be designated ('genius' is a word some people might prefer). For here is to be found the poet, many of whose works are still well-known today; the calligrapher, who through his secretary Sydney Cockerell was to influence the early course of the revival of that art in the next century; and lastly the maker of fine books, who by his whole attitude to the art of the book, has had a profound and lasting influence on twentieth-century book design.

BIBLIOGRAPHY

The Collected Works of William Morris. With introductions by his daughter May Morris. Vol. IX: *Love is Enough; Poems by the Way;* 1911.

The Life of William Morris, by J. W. Mackail. World's Classics edition, 1950.

'William Morris, calligrapher', by Joseph Dunlap. In *William Morris and the Art of the Book*, Pierpont Morgan Library, New York, 1976.

A BOOK OF VERSE
BY
WILLIAM MORRIS
WRITTEN IN LONDON
1870

A TABLE OF CONTENTS

A BOOK OF VERSE

THE TWO SIDES OF THE RIVER

THE YOUTHS

O winter, O white winter, wert thou gone
No more within the wilds were I alone
Leaping with bent bow over stock and stone!

No more alone my love the lamp should burn,
Watching the weary spindle twist and turn,
Or o'er the web hold back her tears and yearn:
O winter, O white winter, wert thou gone!

THE MAIDENS

Sweet thoughts fly swiftlier than the drifting snow,
And with the twisting thread sweet longings grow,
And o'er the web sweet pictures come and go
For no white winter are we long alone.

2

THE TWO SIDES OF THE RIVER

THE YOUTHS

O stream so changed, what hast thou done to me,
That I thy glittering ford no more can see
Wreathing with white her fair feet lovingly?

See, in the rain she stands, and, looking down
With frightened eyes upon thy whirlpools brown
Drops to her feet again her girded gown.
O hurrying turbid stream, what hast thou done?

THE MAIDENS

The clouds lift, telling of a happier day
When through the thin stream I shall take my way,
Girt round with gold, and garlanded with may
What rushing stream can keep us long alone?

THE YOUTHS

O burning Sun, O master of unrest
Why must we, toiling, cast away the best,
Now, when the bird sleeps by her empty nest?

See, with my garland lying at her feet,
In lonely labour stands mine own, my sweet
Above the quern half-filled with half-ground wheat.
O red taskmaster that thy flames were done!

3

THE TWO SIDES OF THE RIVER

THE MAIDENS

O love, to-night across the half shorn plain
Shall I not go to meet the yellow wain,
A look of love at end of toil to gain?
What flaming sun can keep us long alone?

THE YOUTHS

Tomorrow, said I is grape-gathering o'er
Tomorrow, and our loves are twinned no more —
Tomorrow came, to bring us woe and war.

What have I done, that I should stand with these
Hearkening the dread shouts borne upon the breeze
While she, far-off, sits weeping neath her trees?
Alas, O kings, what is it ye have done?

THE MAIDENS

Come love, delay not, come, and slay my dread!
Already is the banquet-table spread;
In the cool chamber flower-strewn is my bed:
Come love what king shall keep us long alone?

THE YOUTHS

O city city, open thou thy gate!
See, with life snatched from out the hand of fate,
How on thy glittering triumph I must wait!

4

THE TWO SIDES OF THE RIVER

Are not her hands stretched out to me? her eyes,
Grow they not weary as each new hope dies,
And lone before her still the long road lies
O golden city, fain would I be gone!

THE MAIDENS

Ah thou art happy, amid shouts and songs
And all that unto congering men belongs
Night hath no fear for me, and day no wrongs
What brazen city-gates can keep us lone?

THE YOUTHS

O long long road, how bare thou art, and grey!
Hill after hill thou climbest, and the day
Is ended now, O moonlit endless way.

And she is standing where the rushes grow,
And still with white hand shades her anxious brow,
Though neath the world the sun is fallen now
O dreary road, when will thy leagues be done?

THE MAIDENS

O tremblest thou, grey road, or do my feet
Tremble with joy, thy flinty face to meet?
Because my love's eyes soon mine eyes shall greet
No heart thou hast to keep us long alone

THE TWO SIDES OF THE RIVER

THE YOUTHS

O wilt thou ne'er depart, thou heavy night?
When will thy slaying bring on the morning bright,
That leads my weary feet to my delight

Why lingerest thou, filling with wandering fears
My lone love's tired heart; her eyes with tears
For thoughts like sorrow for the vanished years?
Weaver of ill thoughts, when wilt thou begone?

THE MAIDENS

Love, to the east are thine eyes turned as mine
In patient watching for the night's decline?
And hast thou noted this grey widening line?
Can any darkness keep us long alone?

THE YOUTHS

O day, O day, is it a little thing
That thou so long unto thy life must cling,
Because I gave thee such a welcoming?

I called thee King of all felicity
I praised thee, that thou broughtest joy so nigh
Thine hours are turned to years, thou wilt not die
O day so longed for, would that thou wert gone

THE TWO SIDES OF THE RIVER

THE MAIDENS

The light fails, love; the long day soon shall be
Nought but a pensive happy memory
Blessed for the tales it told to thee and me.
How hard it was, O love, to be alone.

the end of the
TWO SIDES OF THE
RIVER.

THE SHOWS OF MAY.

I

O love, this morn, when the sweet nightingale
Had so long finished all he had to say
That thou hadst slept, and sleep had told her tale,
And midst a peaceful dream had stolen away
In fragrant dawning of the first of May,
Didst thou see aught, didst thou hear voices sing
Ere to the risen sun the bells gan ring?

II

For then, methought, the Lord of Love went by,
To take possession of his flowery throne,
Ringed round with youths and maids and minstrelsy
A little while I sighed to find him gone
A little while the dawning was alone
And the light gathered; then I held my breath
And shuddered at the sight of Eld and Death

III

Alas, Love passed me in the twilight dun,
His music hushed the wakening ousels song,
But on these twain bright shone the golden sun
And o'er their heads the brown birds' tune was strong
As shivering, twixt the trees they stole along
None noted aught their noiseless passing by,
The World had quite forgotten it must die.

THE FEARS OF JUNE

I

Fair was the morn today, the blossoms' scent
Floated across the fresh grass, and the bees,
With low vexed song from rose to lily went,
A gentle wind was in the heavy trees,
And thine eyes shone with joyous memories;
Fair was the early morn, and fair wert thou
And I was happy — Ah, be happy now!

II

Peace and content without us, love within
That hour there was; now thunder and wild rain
Have wrapped the cowering world, and foolish sin
And nameless pride have made us wise in vain:
Ah love! although the morn shall come again,
And on new rosebuds the new sun shall smile
Can we regain what we have lost meanwhile?

III

Even now the west grows clear of storm and threat,
But midst the lightening did the fair sun die.
Ah he shall rise again for ages yet,
He cannot waste his life; but thou and I —
Who knows if next morn this felicity
My lips may feel, or if thou still shalt live
This seal of love renewed once more to give?

THE HOPES OF OCTOBER.

I

O love, turn from the unchanging sea, and gaze
Down these grey slopes upon the year grown old,
A dying mid the autumn-scented haze
That hangeth o'er the hollow of the wold,
Where the wind-bitten ancient elms enfold
Grey church, long barn, orchard, and red-roofed stead
Wrought in dead days for men a long while dead

II

Come down, O love; may not our hands still meet
Since still we live today, forgetting June
Forgetting May, deeming October sweet—
O hearken, hearken! through the afternoon
The grey tower sings a strange old tinkling tune.
Sweet, sweet and sad, the toiling year's last breath,
Too satiate of life to strive with death.

III

And we too—will it not be soft and kind,
The rest from life, from patience, and from pain,
The rest from bliss we know not when we find,
The rest from love, that ne'er the end can gain?
Hark, how the tune swells, that erewhile did wane!
Look up love!—ah, cling close, and never move!
How can I have enough of life and love?

THE WEARINESS OF NOVEMBER.

I

Are thine eyes weary? is thy heart too sick
To struggle any more with doubt, and thought
Whose formless veil draws darkening now and thick
Across thee e'en as smoke-tinged mist-wreaths, brought
Down a fair dale, to make it blind and nought?
Art thou so weary that no world there seems
Beyond these four walls, hung with pain and dreams?

II

Look out upon the real world, where the moon,
Half-way twixt root and crown of these high trees,
Turns the dead midnight into dreamy noon,
Silent and full of wonders; for the breeze
Died at the sunset, and no images,
No hopes of day are left in sky or earth—
Is it not fair, and of most wondrous worth?

III

Yea I have looked, and seen November there;
The changeless seal of change it seemed to be
Fair death of things, that living once, were fair;
Bright sign of loneliness too great for me;
Strange image of the dread eternity;
In whose void patience how can these have part,
These outstretched feverish hands, this restless heart?

LOVE FULFILLED.

HAST thou longed through weary days
For the sight of one loved face,
Hast thou cried aloud for rest,
Mid the pain of sundering hours,
Cried aloud for sleep and death
Since the sweet unhoped for best
Was a shadow and a breath —
O, long now, for no fear lowers
O'er these faint feet-kissing flowers
O, rest now; and yet in sleep
All thy longing shalt thou keep.

Thou shalt rest, and have no fear
Of a dull awaking near,
Of a life for ever blind,
Uncontent and waste and wide.
Thou shalt wake, and think it sweet
That thy love is near and kind
Sweeter still for lips to meet;
Sweetest, that thine heart doth hide
Longing all unsatisfied
With all longing's answering
Howsoever close ye cling

LOVE FULFILLED.

Thou rememberest how of old
Een thy very pain grew cold,
How thou mightst not measure bliss
Een when eyes and hands drew nigh.
Thou rememberest all regret
For the scarce remembered kiss,
The lost dream of how they met,
Mouths once parched with misery.
Then seemed Love born but to die,
Now unrest, pain, bliss are one,
Love, unhidden and alone.

REST FROM SEEKING.

O WEARY seeker over land and sea
O heart that cravest love perpetually,
Nor knowst his name, come now at last to me!

Come, thirst of love thy lips too long have borne
Hunger of love thy heart hath long outworn;
Speech hadst thou but to call thyself forlorn.

The seeker finds now, the parched lips are led
To sweet full streams, the hungry heart is fed
And song springs up from moans of sorrow dead.

Draw nigh, draw nigh, and tell me of thy tale;
In words grown sweet since all the woe did fail
Show me wherewith thou didst thy woe bewail.

Draw nigh, draw nigh beloved! think of these
Who stand about, as well-wrought images,
Earless and eyeless as the whispering trees.

I think the sky calls living none but three.
The God that looketh thence, and thee and me;
And He made us, but we made Love to be.

14

REST FROM SEEKING

Think not of Time then, for thou shalt not die,
How soon soever shall the World go by,
And nought be left but God and thou and I.

And yet O love, why makest thou delay?
Life comes not till thou comest, and the day
That knows no end may yet be cast away.

MISSING

UPON an eve I sat me down and wept,
Because the world to me seemed nowise good;
Still autumn was it, and the meadows slept,
The misty hills dreamed, and the silent wood
Seemed listening to the sorrow of my mood:
I knew not if the earth with me did grieve,
Or if it mocked my grief that bitter eve.

Then twixt my tears a maiden did I see
Who drew anigh me o'er the leaf-strewn grass,
Then stood and gazed upon me pityfully
With grief-worn eyes, until my woe did pass
From me to her, and tearless now I was,
And she mid tears was asking me of one
She long had sought unaided and alone.

I knew not of him, and she turned away
Into the dark wood, and my own great pain
Still held me there, till dark had slain the day,
And perished at the grey dawn's hand again;
Then from the wood a voice cried: "Ah, in vain
In vain I seek thee, O thou bitter-sweet!
In what lone land are set thy longed-for feet?"

MISSING

Then I looked up, and lo, a man there came
From midst the trees, and stood regarding me
Until my tears were dried for very shame;
Then he cried out; "O mourner, where is she
Whom I have sought o'er every land and sea?
I love her, and she loveth me, and still
We meet no more than green hill meeteth hill."

With that he passed on sadly, and I knew,
That these had met, and missed in the dark night,
Blinded by blindness of the world untrue,
That hideth love, and maketh wrong of right.
Then midst my pity for their lost delight,
Yet more with barren longing I grew weak,
Yet more I mourned that I had none to seek.

PROLOGUE TO THE VOLSUNG TALE.

O HEARKEN ye who speak the English Tongue,
How in a waste land ages long ago
The very heart of the North bloomed into song
After long brooding o'er this tale of woe!
Hearken, and marvel, how it might be so,
How such a sweetness so well crowned could be
Betwixt the ice-hills and the cold grey sea.

Nay rather, marvel not that those should cling
Unto the thought of great lives past away,
Whom God has stripped so bare of everything
Save the one longing to wear through their day
In fearless wise; the hope the Gods to stay,
When at that last tide gathered wrong and hate
Shall meet blind yearning on the fields of fate.

Yea, in the first grey dawning of our race
This ruth-crowned tangle to sad hearts was dear.
Then rose a seeming sun, the lift gave place
Unto a seeming heaven, far-off but clear;
But that passed too, and afternoon is here;
Nor was the morn so fruitful or so long
But we may hearken when ghosts moan of wrong.

PROLOGUE TO THE VOLSUNG TALE.

For as amid the clatter of the town
When eve comes on with unabated noise,
The soaring wind will sometimes drop adown
And bear unto our chamber the sweet voice
Of bells, that mid the swallows do rejoice
Half heard to make us sad; so we awhile
With echoed grief life's tumult may beguile.

Naught vague, naught base our tale, that seems to say:
Be wide-eyed, kind, curse not the hand that smites
Curse not the kindness of a past good day,
Or hope of love: cast by all earth's delights
For very Love: through weary days and nights
Abide thou, striving, howsoe'er in vain,
The inmost love of one more heart to gain.

So draw ye round and hearken, English Folk
Unto the best tale pity ever wrought,
Of how from dark to dark bright Sigurd broke
Of Brynhild's glorious soul by love distraught,
Of Gudrun's weary wandering unto naught
Of utter Love defeated utterly
Of Grief too strong to give Love time to die.

LOVE AND DEATH

IN the white-flowered hawthorn brake
Love be merry for my sake;
Twine the blossoms in my hair
Kiss me where I am most fair
Kiss me, sweet, for who knoweth
What thing cometh after death!

NAY thy garlanded gold hair
Hides thee where thou art most fair,
Hides the rose-tinged hills of snow—
O my love I hold thee now!
Kiss me, sweet, for who knoweth
What thing cometh after death!

SHALL we weep for a dead day,
Or set sorrow in our way?
Hidden in my golden hair
Wilt thou weep that the days wear?
Kiss me, sweet, for who knoweth
What thing cometh after death!

LOVE AND DEATH

WEEP O love the days that flit
Now, while I can feel thy breath;
Then may I remember it
Sad and old, and near my death
Kiss me sweet, for who knoweth
What thing cometh after death!

GUILEFUL LOVE.

LOVE set me in a flowery garden fair
Love showed me many marvels moving there
Love said Take these, if nought thy soul doth dare
To feel my fiery hand upon thine heart,
Take these, and live, and lose the better part.

Love showed me Death, and said, Make no delay;
Love showed me Change, and said, Joy ebbs away;
Love showed me Eld amid regrets grown grey—
I laughed for joy, and round his heart I clung,
Sickened and swooned by bitter-sweetness stung.

But I awoke at last, and born again
Laid eager hands upon unrest and pain,
And wrapped myself about with longing vain:
Ah, better still and better all things grew,
As more the root and heart of Love I knew.

O Love Love Love, what is it thou hast done?
All pains, all fears I knew, save only one;
Where is the fair earth now, where is the sun?
Thou didst not say my Love might never move
Her eyes, her hands, her lips to bless my love.

SUMMER NIGHT.

O LOVE O love though thy lids are shut close,
Yet hearken the sweet-breathed rustling rose!

Why liest thou sleeping, yet red with shame
While the harp-strings tremble to hear thy name?

Hearken the harp in a trembling hand!
Hearken soft speech of a far off land!

O my love, if thou hearest my foot-steps anear
Thy very breathing methinks I may hear

O my sweet, is it true that we are alone,
The grey leaves a-quiver twixt us and the moon

O me, the love, the love in thine eyes,
Now the night is a-dying as all life dies!

Art thou come, swift end of beginning of bliss?
O my sweet! O thine eyes, O thy hands O thy kiss!

HOPE DIETH LOVE LIVETH

STRONG are thine arms O love, and strong
Thine heart to live and love and long
But thou art wed to grief and wrong:
Live then and long, though hope is dead!

Live on and labour through the years!
Make pictures through the mist of tears
Of unforgotten happy fears,
That crossed the time ere hope was dead.

Draw near the place where once we stood
Amid delights swift-rushing flood,
And we and all the world seemed good
Nor needed hope now cold and dead.

Dream in the dawn I come to thee
Weeping for things that may not be!
Dream that thou layest lips on me!
Wake, wake to clasp hopes body dead!

Count oer and oer, and one by one
The minutes of the happy sun
That while agone on kissed lips shone.
Count on, rest not for hope is dead.

24

HOPE DIETH LOVE LIVETH

Weep, though no hairsbreadth thou shalt move
The settled earth, the heavens above
By all the bitterness of love!
Weep and cease not, now hope is dead!

Sighs rest thee not, tears bring no ease,
Life hath no joy and Death no peace:
The years change not, though they decrease
For hope is dead, for hope is dead!

Speak, love, I listen: far away
I bless thy tremulous lips, that say—
'Mock not the afternoon of day
Mock not the tide when hope is dead!'

I bless thee, O my love, who say'st:
'Mock not the thistle-cumbered waste!
I hold Love's hand, and make no haste
Down the long way, now hope is dead.

'With other names do we name pain,
The long years wear our hearts in vain.
Mock not our loss grown into gain

HOPE DIETH LOVE LIVETH

Mock not our lost hope lying dead.

'Our eyes gaze for no morning-star
No glimmer of the dawn afar;
Full silent wayfarers we are
Since ere the noon-tide hope lay dead.

'Behold with lack of happiness
The Master, Love our hearts did bless
Lest we should think of him the less—
Love dieth not, though hope is dead!'

LOVE ALONE

O FAR away to seek, close-hid for heart to find,
O hard to cast away, impossible to bind
A pain when found and held, a pain when fallen away,
Still joy or pain or anguish, be nigh us, Love, today!

Sweet was the summer day, before thou camest here:
But never sweet to me, and Death was drawing near—
Is it summer still? what means the ill word Death?
What means the utter joy thy mouth, Love, promiseth?

Wherefore must thou babble of my being once alone?
What is this idle word, that thou mayst yet begone?
Laugh laugh, Love, as I laugh when mine own love kisseth me,
And saith no more of joy 'twixt lips and lips shall be.

O Love thou hast slain Time; how shall he live again
O Love thou hast slain rest and we bless thy sleepless pain.
Hope and Fear have slain each other, Doubt forgetteth all he said.
Death in some place forgotten, lingering and half-dead.

27

LOVE ALONE

When my hand forgets her cunning I will loose thee Love, and pray,
—Ah, and pray to what?— for a never-ending day
Wherein we twain may sit, parted undying still,
With thoughts of the old story, our sundered hearts to fill.

28

MEETING IN WINTER

WINTER in the world it is
Round about the unhoped kiss
Whose shadow I have long moaned o'er
Round about the longing sore,
That the touch of thee shall turn
Into joy too deep to burn.

Round thine eyes and round thy mouth
Passeth no murmur of the south
When my lips a little while
Leave thy quivering tender smile,
As we twain, hand touching hand,
Once again together stand.

Sweet is that as all is sweet,
For the white drift shalt thou meet
Kind and cold-cheeked, and mine own,
Wrapped about with deepfurred gown
In the broad-wheeled chariot;
Then the north shall spare us not,
The wide-reaching waste of snow
Wilder, lonelier yet shall grow
As the reddened sun falls down.

MEETING IN WINTER.

But the warders of the town,
When they flash the torches out
O'er the snow amid their doubt,
And their eyes at last behold
Thy red-litten hair of gold,
Shall they open, or in fear
Cry ; Alas, what cometh here ?
Whence hath come this heavenly one
To tell of all the world undone ?

They shall open and we shall see
The long street litten scantily
By the stream of light before
The guest-halls half open door,
And our horses bells shall cease
As we gain the place of peace :
Thou shalt tremble, as at last
The worn threshold is o'erpast,
And the fire-light blindeth thee ;
Trembling shalt thou cling to me
As the sleepy merchants stare
At thy cold hands, slim and fair,
Thy soft eyes and happy lips
Worth all lading of all ships

30

MEETING IN WINTER.

O my love, how over-sweet
That first kissing of thy feet,
When the fire is sunk alow,
And the hall made empty now
Groweth solemn dim and vast!

O my love, the night shall last
Longer than men tell thereof
Laden with our lonely love!

A GARDEN BY THE SEA

I KNOW a little garden-close,
Set thick with lily and red rose,
Where I would wander if I might
From dewy morn to dewy night
And have one with me wandering

And though within it no birds sing,
And though no pillared house is there
And though the apple-boughs are bare
Of fruit and blossom, would to God
Her feet upon the green grass trod
And I beheld them as before.

There comes a murmur from the shore,
And in the close two fair streams are,
Drawn from the purple hills afar
Drawn down unto the restless sea:
Dark hills whose heath-bloom feeds no bee,
Dark shore no ship has ever seen,
Tormented by the billows green
Whose murmur comes unceasingly
Unto the place for which I cry

For which I cry both day and night,

A GARDEN BY THE SEA

For which I let slip all delight,
Whereby I grow both deaf and blind,
Careless to win, unskilled to find,
And quick to lose what all men seek.

Yet tottering as I am and weak
Still have I left a little breath
To seek within the jaws of death
An entrance to that happy place,
To seek the unforgotten face,
Once seen once kissed, once reft from me
Anigh the murmuring of the sea

THE BALLAD OF CHRISTINE.

Of silk my gown was shapen,
Scarlet they did on me
Then to the sea-strand was I borne
And laid in a bark of the sea.
O, well would I from the World away

But on the sea I might not drown,
To me was God so good,
The billows bore me up aland
Where grew the fair green-wood

There came a knight a riding by
With three swains along the way
And took me up, the little-one
On the sea-strand as I lay

He took me up, and bore me home
To the house that was his own,
And there so long I bode with him
That I was his love alone.

But the very first night we lay abed
Befell this sorrow and harm,
That thither came the king's ill men,

THE BALLAD OF CHRISTINE.

And slew him on mine arm.

There slew they the King Ethelbert
Two of his swains slew they
But the third sailed swiftly from the land
For ever to bide away.

O, wavering hope of this world's bliss,
How shall men trow in thee?
My grove of gems is gone away,
For mine eyen no more to see!

Each hour that this my life shall last
Remembereth him alone
Such heavy sorrow lies on me
For our meeting time agone. —

Ah, early of a morning-tide
Men cry, Christine the Fair,
Art thou well content with that true-love
Thou sittest loving there?

O yea, so well I love him,
So dear to my heart is he,

THE BALLAD OF CHRISTINE.

That the very God of Heaven aloft
Worshippeth him and me.

All the red gold that I have
Well would I give today,
Only for this and nothing else,
From the World to win away

Ah, of all folk upon the earth
Keep thou thy ruddy gold,
And love withal the mighty lord
Who wedded thee of old.
O well would I from the World away

TO GRETTIR ASMUNDSON.

A LIFE scarce worth the living; a poor fame
Scarce worth the winning, in a wretched land,
Where fear and pain go upon either hand,
As toward the end men fare without an aim
Unto the dull grey dusk from whence they came—
Let them alone, the unshadowed shear rocks stand
Over the twilight graves of that poor band,
Who count so little in the Great World's Game!

Nay, with the dead I deal not; this man lives,
And that, which carried him through good and ill,
Stern against Fate, while his voice echoed still
From rock to rock, now he lies silent strives
With wasting Time, and through its long lapse gives
Another friend to me, lifes void to fill.

THE SON'S SORROW

THE king has asked of his son so good —
Why art thou hushed and heavy of mood
O fair and sweet to ride abroad!

Thou playest not, and thou laughest not,
All thy good game is clean forgot —

Sit thou beside me, father dear,
And the tale of my sorrow shalt thou hear.

Thou sentest me into a far off land
Thou gavest me into a good earl's hand

Now this good earl had daughters seven
The fairest of maidens under the heaven.

One brought me my meat when I should dine
One shaped and sewed my raiment fine.

One washed and combed my yellow hair
And one I fell to loving there

Befell it on so fair a day
That folk must win them sport and play

THE SON'S SORROW

Down in a dale my horse bound I
My saddle bound right speedily

Bright was her face as the flickering flame
When to my saddlebow she came

Beside my saddlebow she stood —
O knight, to flee with thee were good! —

Kind was my horse, and good to aid,
My love upon his back I laid.

Then from the garth I rode away
And none were ware of us that day

But as we rode along the sand
There lay a barge beside the land.

So in that barge did we depart
And rowed away right glad of heart

When we came to the dark wood and the shade
To raise the tent my true-love bade.

THE SON'S SORROW

Three sons my true-love bore me there,
And syne she died, who was so dear.

A grave I made her with my sword
And with my shield the mould I poured;

First in the mould I laid my love
Then all my sons her breast above.

And I without must lie alone,
So homeward thenceforth gat I gone—

No man any more shall rise on his feet
To love that Love, to woo that sweet.

Five leagues away the mould below
She trembled with his weary woe.
O fair and sweet to ride abroad!

THE LAPSE OF THE YEAR

SPRING am I, too soft of heart
Much to speak ere I depart:
Ask the summer-tide to prove
The abundance of my love

SUMMER looked for long am I
Much shall change or ere I die
Prithee take it not amiss
Though I weary thee with bliss!

Laden AUTUMN here I stand,
Weak of heart and worn of hand;
Speak the word that sets me free,
Nought but rest seems good to me

Ah, shall WINTER mend your case?
Set your teeth the wind to face,
Beat the snow down, tread the frost,
All is gained when all is lost.

SUNDERING SUMMER.

FAIR is the night and fair the day
Now April is forgot of May,
Now into June May falls away.
Fair day, fair night, O give me back
The tide that all fair things did lack
Except my Love except my Sweet!

Blow back O wind, thou art not kind
Though thou be soft: thou hast no mind
Her hair about my Sweet to wind.
O flowery sward, though thou be bright
I praise thee not for thy delight,
Thou hast not kissed her silver feet.

Thou knowest Her not, O rustling tree,
What dost thou then to shadow me
With boughs Her eyen did never see?
O flowers, in vain ye bow adown,
Ye have not felt Her odorous gown
Brush past your leaves my lips to meet.

Flow on great river; thou mayst deem
That far away, a summer stream
Thou sawest her limbs amid thee gleam,

SUNDERING SUMMER.

And, kissing foot, and kissing knee
Passed on to the forgetful sea—
Yet with naught true thou wilt me greet.

And thou, that men called by my name
O helpless one, hast thou no shame
That thou must even now seem the same
As while agone, as while agone,
When thou and She stood close alone,
And hands and lips and tears did meet.

Grow weak and pine lie down to die,
O body, in thy misery
Because short time and sweet goes by
O foolish heart, how weak thou art!
Break, break, because thou needs must part
From thine own Love, from thine own Sweet.

TO THE MUSE OF THE NORTH

O THOU who swayest the sad northern song,
Thy right hand full of smiting and of wrong,
Thy left hand holding pity, and thy breast
Heaving with hope of that so certain rest,
Thou with the grey eyes kind and unafraid,
The soft lips trembling not that they have said
The doom of the World and those that dwell therein,
The lips that smile not though thy children win
The fated Love, that earns the fated Death —
Borne down the balmy freshness of thy breath
Let some word reach my ears and touch my heart,
That, if it may be, I may have a part
In that sweet sorrow of thy children dead
That smote the soul, and bowed adown the head,
Whitened the hair, made Life an eager dream,
And Death the murmuring of a peaceful stream
But left no blemish on those souls of thine
Whose fairness through the dim World yet doth shine

O Mother and Love and Sister all in one,
Come thou, for am I not enough alone
That thou thine arms about my heart shouldst throw,
And wrap me in the griefs of Long Ago?

44

LONELY LOVE AND LOVELESS DEATH

O HAVE I been hearkening
To some dread new-comer?
What chain is it bindeth,
What curse is anigh,
That the World is a-darkening
Amidmost the summer,
That the soft sunset blindeth
And Death standeth by?

Doth it wane, is it going,
Is it gone by for ever,
The life that seemed round me
The longing I sought?
Has it turned to undoing,
That constant endeavour
To kind love that bound me
To hold all it brought?

I beheld till beholding
Grew pain thrice told over;
I hearkened till hearing
Grew woe beyond speech;
I dreamed of enfolding
Arms blessing the lover

LONELY LOVE AND LOVELESS DEATH

Till the dream past all bearing
The dark void did reach.

Beaten back, ever smitten
By pains that none knoweth,
Did love ever languish
Did hope ever die?
I know not, but litten
By the light that love showeth
I beheld her through anguish
Never lost, never nigh.

I know not: but never
The day was without her,
I know not; but morning
Still woke me to her;
The miles that might sever
All faces about her
Weary days, and self-scorning—
Ah easy to bear!

Look back, while grown colder,
The sunless day lingers,
And the tree-tops are stirring

46

LONELY LOVE AND LOVELESS DEATH

With the last wind of day—
If thou didst behold her
If thine hand touched her fingers
If her breath thou wert hearing
What words wouldst thou say?

Words meet for the hearkening
Of Death the new-comer;
For the new bond that bindeth,
The new pain anigh:
For the World is a-darkening
Amidmost the summer,
Death sickeneth and blindeth
No love standeth by.

BIRTH OF JUNE

HOW the wind howls this morn,
About the end of May
And drives June on apace
To mock the World forlorn,
And the Worlds joy past away,
And my unlonged for face!

The Worlds joy past away—
For no more may I deem
That any heart is glad
To see the break of day
Sunder the tangled dream
Wherein no grief it had.

Ah, through the tangled dream
Where others have no grief
Ever it fares with me
That fears and treasons stream;
And sleep slays all belief
Of what I hoped might be.

Sleep slayeth all belief,
Until the hapless light
Wakes at the birth of June

BIRTH OF JUNE

More lying tales to weave,
More love in woes despite
More hope to perish soon.

More love in woes despite—
Then, O tongue, hold thy peace!
Be silent thankless heart,
Nor wish the World were bright
Nor wish for Autumn's ease!
Thou hast the better part.

PRAISE OF VENUS

BEFORE our lady came on earth
Little there was of joy or mirth
About the borders of the sea
The sea-folk wandered wearily,
About the wintry river-side
The weary fishers would abide

Alone within the weaving room
The girls would sit before the loom
And sing no song and play no play

Alone from dawn to hot mid-day
From mid-day unto evening
The men afield would work, nor sing
Mid weary thoughts of man and God
Before thy feet the wet ways trod

Unkissed the merchant bore his care
Unkissed the knights went out to war,
Unkissed the mariner came home,
Unkissed the minstrel men must roam

Or in the stream the maids would stare
Nor know why they were shapen fair

Their yellow locks, their bosoms white
Their limbs well wrought for all delight,
Seemed fruitless things that waited death
As hopeless as the flowers beneath
The weariness of unkissed feet.

THEREFORE O Venus well may we
Praise the green ridges of the sea
O'er which upon a happy day
Thou cam'st to take our shame away
Well may we praise the curdling foam
Amidst the which thy feet did bloom,
Flowers of the Gods; the yellow sand
They kissed betwixt the sea and land
The bee-beset ripe seeded grass
Through which thy fine limbs first did pass;
The purple-dusted butterfly
First blown against thy quivering thigh;
The first red rose that touched thy side
And overblown and fainting died;
The flickering of the orange shade
Where first in sleep thy limbs were laid;
The happy day's sweet life and death
Whose air first caught thy balmy breath:—

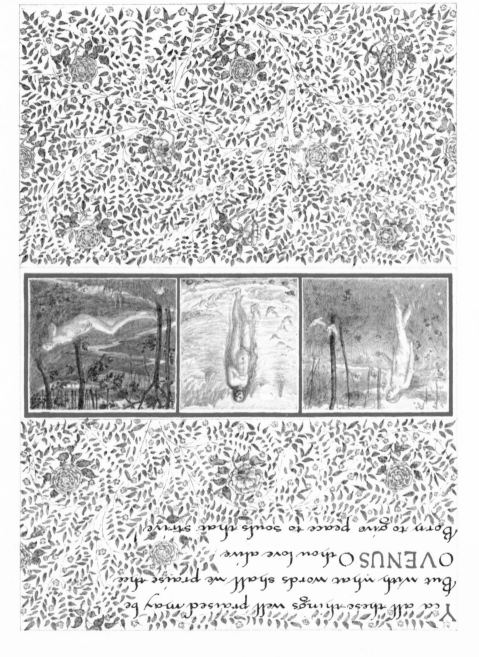

PRAISE OF VENUS

Yea all these things well praised may be
But with what words shall we praise thee
O VENUS O thou love alive
Born to give peace to souls that strive!

As to those who have had a hand in making this book, Edward Burne Jones painted the picture on page 1: the other pictures were all painted by Charles F Murray, but the minstrel figures on the title-page, and the figures of Spring Summer and Autumn on page 40, he did from my drawings.

As to the pattern-work, George Wardle drew in all the ornament on the first ten pages, and I coloured it; he also did all the coloured letters both big and little; the rest of the ornament I did, together with all the writing.

Also I made all the verses; but two poems, the Ballad of Christine, and the Son's Sorrow I translated out of Icelandic.

William Morris
26 Queen Sq: Bloomsbury London
August 26th 1870.